SPACE MISSIONS™

The Apollo 11 Mission
The First Man to Walk on the Moon

Helen Zelon

The Rosen Publishing Group's
PowerKids Press™
New York

For David Sasson, rocket boy, beloved son

Published in 2002 by The Rosen Publishing Group, Inc.
29 East 21st Street, New York, NY 10010

First Edition

Book Design: Michael de Guzman
Project Editors: Jennifer Landau, Jason Moring, Jennifer Quasha

Photo Credits: p. 4 (President Kennedy) © Bettmann/CORBIS, (Aldrin, Armstrong, and Collins) © Hulton-Deutsch Collection/CORBIS; pp. 6, 7, 8 (background and inset) © Photri-Microstock; p. 10 © Bettmann/CORBIS; p. 11 (Buzz Aldrin aboard the lunar module), (Neil Armstrong aboard the Eagle) Digital image © 1996 CORBIS; Original image courtesy of NASA/CORBIS; p. 12 © NASA/Roger Ressmeyer/CORBIS; p. 15 (Earth rising on Moon horizon) © CORBIS, (lunar module in space) Digital image © 1996 CORBIS; Original image courtesy of NASA/CORBIS; p. 16 (astronaut taking moon samples) Digital image © 1996 CORBIS; Original image courtesy of NASA/CORBIS, (Aldrin descends from lunar module) © CORBIS; p. 19 (bag of equipment) Digital image © 1996 CORBIS; original image courtesy of NASA/CORBIS, (American flag) © CORBIS, (Moon plaque) © Bettmann/CORBIS, p. 20 Digital image © 1996 CORBIS; Original image courtesy of NASA/CORBIS.

Zelon, Helen.
The Apollo 11 mission : the first man to walk on the moon / Helen Zelon.
    p. cm. — (Space missions)
ISBN 0-8239-5772-1 (library binding)
1. Project Apollo (U.S.)—Juvenile literature. 2. Apollo 11 (Spacecraft)—Juvenile literature. 3. Space flight to the
moon—Juvenile literature. [1. Project Apollo (U.S.) 2. Apollo 11 (Spacecraft) 3. Space flight to the moon.] I. Title. II. Series.
    TL789.8.U6 A694 2001
    629.45'4'0973—dc21

                                                                                        00-013043

Manufactured in the United States of America

Contents

NEIL A. ARMSTRONG

MICHAEL C.

Reach for the Moon

During the twentieth century, scientists and engineers made airplanes, rockets, and spacecraft that helped explore the sky above Earth. In 1961, President John F. Kennedy set a goal for American astronauts to land on the Moon before 1970. Project Mercury was the first U.S. space program. It showed that astronauts could **orbit** Earth and safely return home. Project Gemini followed Mercury. The Gemini astronauts went on long and **complicated** missions. The third space program was Apollo. Apollo's goal was to land American astronauts on the Moon. By 1969, the Apollo 11 astronauts Michael Collins, Neil A. Armstrong, and Edwin E. "Buzz" Aldrin were ready to explore the Moon.

Above: *This picture shows President John F. Kennedy announcing the start of the U.S. space program in 1961. Below (from left to right): Astronauts Buzz Aldrin, Neil Armstrong, and Michael Collins in 1969.*

The *Eagle* and the Spider

A powerful Saturn V rocket took Apollo 11 astronauts Armstrong, Aldrin, and Collins into space. The Saturn V rocket stood 360 feet (110 m) high and weighed more than 6 million pounds (2.7 million kg)! Its immense power was needed to launch the astronauts and their spacecraft with enough force to reach the Moon.

The outside of the rocket was covered with a thin, metal skin, like the skin that covers your body. The

↑
Above: *The Apollo 11 spacecraft stands tall on the launchpad.*

metal skin was light but very strong. It could survive the blasting fires of a launch and space travel. The Apollo 11 spacecraft had two important parts. The **command module** was shaped like a cone. The pointed end faced up, toward the tip of the rocket. The crew lived and worked in its broad, bell-shaped base. The **lunar module** had two jobs. It would land on the Moon and would bring back the astronauts to the command module. It was nicknamed the *Eagle*. The *Eagle* looked like a big, golden spider.

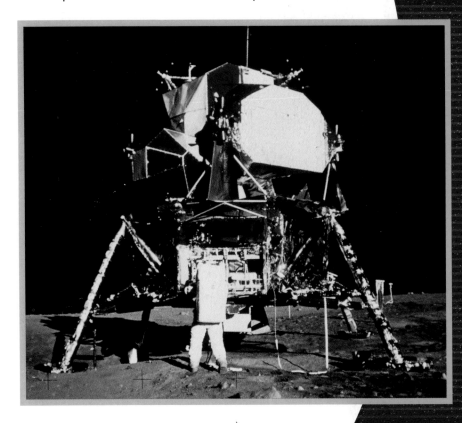

The astronauts nicknamed the lunar module the Eagle, *but it looked more like a big spider.*

Launch into Orbit

Millions of people around the world watched the Apollo 11 launch on July 16, 1969. The Saturn V rocket engines blasted their powerful fire onto the **launchpad**. A flood of thousands of gallons (liters) of water cooled the launchpad after **liftoff**.

Sending a spacecraft to the Moon was like trying to pitch a baseball across a moving home plate. The scientists had to be able to predict where the Moon would be and then aim Apollo 11 to the exact place in the sky. They had to be sure of the correct position. If they were wrong, the astronauts would **bypass** the Moon. The astronauts and the Apollo 11 **space capsule** would float into empty space forever.

← *The large photo shows the Apollo 11 spacecraft at liftoff. The small photo is a view from Apollo 11 of a used stage of the Saturn rocket, falling into the ocean after its fuel has burned away.*

Descent to the Moon

All three Apollo 11 astronauts were busy as they headed for the Moon. Commander Mike Collins was in the command module. He watched the instruments, dials, switches, and displays that kept him on course and in contact with scientists on Earth. Neil Armstrong and Buzz Aldrin left the command module for the small lunar module, which would take them to the Moon's surface. There was no room for Armstrong and Aldrin to sit down in the lunar module. Instead, they floated standing up, held in place by elastic cords

This is a picture of Mike Collins in the command module. ➤

attached to the floor. The lunar module approached the landing site, the Sea of Tranquility. It had looked peaceful from telescopes on Earth, but as the astronauts came closer, they saw that it was full of dangerous boulders. A rough landing could damage the lunar module and end their mission. Neil Armstrong decided to look for safer ground for the descent to the Moon.

This photo shows astronaut Buzz Aldrin in the lunar module.

Astronaut Neil Armstrong is shown in the lunar module.

A Scary Landing

Neil Armstrong and Buzz Aldrin flew the lunar module low over the Moon's surface to search for a safe place to land. They were not sure that there was enough fuel to land at another site. They also had to save enough fuel to leave the Moon once their work was done. The command module was not made to land on the Moon. If Armstrong and Aldrin ran out of fuel, Commander Collins would not be able to rescue them. Suddenly an alarm went off. Most of the lunar module's fuel was gone. If it didn't land in less than 94 seconds, Armstrong and Aldrin would have to return to the command module without landing on the Moon. At last, Neil Armstrong spotted a smooth site. The astronauts landed with only 20 seconds' worth of fuel to spare.

← *This is a picture of the Moon and its craters. Craters are hollow dents in the Moon's surface that look like the inside of a bowl.*

"The *Eagle* Has Landed"

Neil Armstrong radioed to Earth, "The *Eagle* has landed." The scientists and engineers from **Mission Control** signaled back, "Roger."

The astronauts heard cheering at Mission Control. Everyone wanted to celebrate, but the astronauts had work to do. They had to leave the lunar module and walk on the Moon. They had to collect Moon rocks and dust. There were experiments to conduct and **equipment** to set up.

Aldrin and Armstrong were supposed to take a five-hour rest after landing on the Moon, but they were too excited to sleep! Instead, they got ready to explore the Moon's surface. From the lunar module's windows, they saw a blue-green **sphere** in the black sky. It was Earth.

From the lunar module, shown here, the astronauts were able to see Earth. ➡

This picture of Earth was taken from the Moon. ➡

"One Small Step..."

On July 20, 1969, Neil Armstrong became the first man to walk on the Moon. Crawling backward through the *Eagle*'s escape **hatch** in his bulky space suit, Armstrong left the lunar module and climbed down a short ladder to a footpad. "That's one small step for man, one giant leap for mankind," Armstrong said as he stepped onto the Moon's surface. The soil on the Moon was fine and powdery, like gray baby powder. Armstrong's boots left deep, sharp prints. Buzz Aldrin joined him on the Moon's surface about 15 minutes later. Armstrong was taking photographs. Armstrong was so excited that he forgot to ask Aldrin to take his picture, too! The only photos of Armstrong on the Moon show him as a small reflection in Aldrin's gold-plated helmet **visor**.

← *The large picture shows Buzz Aldrin stepping onto the surface of the Moon. In the small picture, Aldrin picks up soil from the Moon.*

On the Moon

On Earth, each astronaut with his equipment weighed 360 pounds (163 kg). On the Moon, the weight was only 60 pounds (27 kg) each. This is because the Moon's **gravity** is much weaker than Earth's. Less gravity makes solid objects weigh less, because less force holds them down to the ground. On the Moon, Armstrong and Aldrin walked, ran, and hopped like kangaroos. They conducted experiments, collected soil samples, and placed an American flag on the Moon.

After 2 hours and 31 minutes on the Moon, Aldrin and Armstrong climbed back up the ladder and into the lunar module. They took one last look at the Moon's surface and closed the hatch. It was time to get ready to return to the command module and then to Earth.

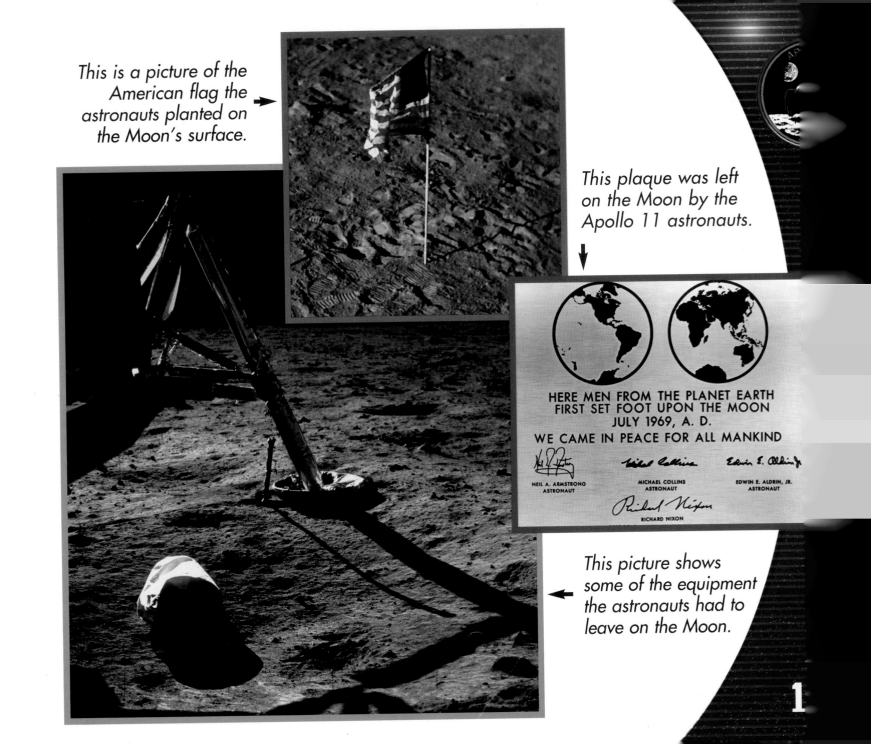

This is a picture of the American flag the astronauts planted on the Moon's surface.

This plaque was left on the Moon by the Apollo 11 astronauts.

HERE MEN FROM THE PLANET EARTH
FIRST SET FOOT UPON THE MOON
JULY 1969, A. D.
WE CAME IN PEACE FOR ALL MANKIND

NEIL A. ARMSTRONG
ASTRONAUT

MICHAEL COLLINS
ASTRONAUT

EDWIN E. ALDRIN, JR.
ASTRONAUT

RICHARD NIXON

This picture shows some of the equipment the astronauts had to leave on the Moon.

Mission Accomplished

Armstrong and Aldrin returned to the Apollo 11 lunar module. They climbed up into the top part of the lunar module, called the **ascent** stage. The ascent stage had a small rocket engine that would take them back to meet Mike Collins in the command module. The *Eagle*'s shiny base is still on the Moon today.

In the ascent stage, Armstrong and Aldrin were nervous. The rocket had enough fuel for only one blast. That one blast was their single chance to return to safety. After 2 hours and 31 minutes on the surface of the Moon, their ascent engine fired. They blasted off.

Commander Collins watched the lunar module's approach. As the two spacecraft met, Collins welcomed his friends back to the command module.

← *In this picture, the lunar module is heading back to meet the command module.*

The World Celebrates the Dream

Four days after Neil Armstrong and Buzz Aldrin became the first men to walk on the Moon, the Apollo 11 spacecraft splashed down into the Atlantic Ocean. The astronauts were rescued by a U.S. Navy carrier called the *Hornet*. All three men were **quarantined** for three weeks because doctors wanted to be sure that they hadn't brought any dangerous **microbes** or germs back to Earth from the Moon. Weeks later, President Nixon honored the astronauts with medals. The Apollo 11 astronauts borrowed the president's airplane, *Air Force One*, for a world tour. They went to 27 cities in 24 countries. Everywhere they went, people honored their courage and celebrated the dream that came true when men walked on the Moon.

Glossary

ascent (uh-SENT) The process of going upward.

bypass (BI-pass) To pass by going around.

command module (kuh-MAND MAH-jool) The area of a space capsule where astronauts live and work.

complicated (KOM-plih-kay-ted) Hard to understand or do.

equipment (ih-KWIP-mint) All of the supplies needed to do an activity.

gravity (GRA-vih-tee) The natural force that causes objects to move or tend to move toward the center of Earth.

hatch (HACH) A doorlike opening in a spacecraft.

launchpad (LAWNCH-pad) The pad from which a spacecraft is sent off into the air.

liftoff (LIFT-ahf) A vertical takeoff by a rocket or aircraft.

lunar module (LOO-ner MAH-jool) The part of the space capsule that lands on the Moon.

microbes (MY-krohbz) Very tiny living things that may carry disease.

Mission Control (MISH-shun kun-TROHL) A group of scientists that controls a space mission from the ground.

orbit (OR-bit) When one body makes a path around another, usually, larger body.

quarantined (KWAR-in-teend) Kept separate from others for fear of spreading illness.

space capsule (SPAYS KAP-sul) A spacecraft.

sphere (SFEER) An object that is shaped like a ball.

visor (VY-zer) A rim that sticks out at the front of a cap.

Index

A

Air Force One, 22
Aldrin, Edwin E.
      "Buzz," 5, 6, 10,
      13, 14, 17, 18,
      21, 22
Armstrong, Neil, 5, 6,
      10, 11, 13, 14,
      17, 18, 21, 22
ascent stage, 21

C

Collins, Commander
      Michael, 5, 6, 10,
      13, 21

command module, 7,
      10, 13, 18, 21

E

Eagle, the, 7, 14, 21

H

Hornet, the, 22

K

Kennedy, President
      John F., 5

L

lunar module, 7, 10,
      11, 13, 14, 18

M

Mission Control, 14
Moon rocks and dust,
      14

P

President Nixon, 22
Project Gemini, 5
Project Mercury, 5

S

Saturn V rocket, 6, 9
Sea of Tranquility, 11
soil on the Moon, 17
space capsule, 9

Web Sites

To find out more about the Apollo 11 Mission and spaceflight, check out these
   Web sites:
      http://spaceflight.nasa.gov
      www.jsc.nasa.gov